THE BREAKUP BREAKTHROUGH JOURNAL

WRITE YOUR WAY BACK TO YOURSELF

AFTER HEARTBREAK

Paige Wilhide

Copyright © 2020 by Paige Wilhide

All rights reserved. No part of this publication may be reproduced, distributed or transmitted in any form or by any means, including photocopying, recording, or other electronic or mechanical methods, without the prior written permission of the publisher, except in the case of brief quotations embodied in critical reviews and certain other noncommercial uses permitted by copyright law. For permission requests, write to the publisher, addressed "Attention: Permissions Coordinator," at hello@breakupbreakthrough.com.

Ordering Information:

Quantity sales. Special discounts are available on quantity purchases by corporations, associations, and others. For details, contact hello@breakupbreakthrough.com.

The Breakup Breakthrough Journal/ Paige Wilhide —1st ed.

ISBN 978-1-953449-04-7

This journal belongs to:

Y ou are perfect, whole, complete, and exactly where you need to be.

You are *not* broken.
You are *not* unlovable.
You are *not* at the end of your journey.

In fact, you're at the beginning of one. Just by showing up and being here right now, you are saying YES to you. So take this moment to celebrate yourself.

I celebrate myself for:

_____

_____

_____

_____

I want to celebrate with you. DM me on Instagram and share what you're celebrating!
@breakupbreakthrough

This journal will walk you through the breakup recovery process, using curated journal prompts and exercises to help you find your way back to yourself. It is designed to guide you, step-by-step, through your healing. So turn the page and let your next chapter begin!

PART ONE:
FEEL YOUR FEELINGS

"It is the tears of your grief that provide the water for the soil of your unfolding and evolving storyline."
- *Regena Thomashauer, aka "Mama Gena"*

You're experiencing a lot of change right now; this breakup isn't want you planned or expected. And with change comes feelings. That's why "feeling your feelings" is the first step on this path. In this part of your journal, you are encouraged to feel the full range of your emotions and grant yourself approval for all of them.

There is nothing bad or wrong or negative about the emotions that are coming through you. Resist your urge to judge them. And keep in mind that what you're feeling is temporary. It will pass. Let yourself go there and feel it fully. And then let it pass.

PERMISSION TO FEEL

Each hour today, write how you're feeling,
followed by, "and that's ok."

(Example: I'm feeling lonely, and that's ok. I'm feeling tired, and that's ok, etc.)

7am

8am

9am

10am

11am

12pm

1pm

2pm

3pm

4pm

5pm

6pm

7pm

8pm

This page is for your sadness

Wet it with your tears, unravel your grief here.

THIS IS HOW I FEEL TODAY...
(draw or write)

THIS PAGE IS FOR YOUR ANGER

Both sides are available to use-- tear it up, burn it, poke holes, scratch it to oblivion.

Don't restrict your anger to this page. Feel free to take a few swings at a pillow and let your voice out!

WHAT MY HEART NEEDS TODAY…

If my emotions could talk, they would say…

HERE'S WHAT I CAN GIVE MYSELF...

HERE'S WHAT I NEED FROM OTHERS...

HERE'S WHAT WOULD FEEL GOOD RIGHT NOW…

My Intuition is telling me...

MOVEMENT MENU

Here are all the ways I like to move my body:

Movement keeps your feelings from getting stuck in your body, alchemizing them into joy, creativity, and power.

Now pick something from this menu and get moving!

PART TWO:
REFLECT ON LESSONS LEARNED

"People are sent into our lives to teach us things that we need to learn about ourselves."

– *Mandy Hale*

A breakup is not worth the suffering if you don't learn from your experience. You have the opportunity here to turn your breakup into a breakthrough and emerge on the other side with more confidence, sparkle, and self-worth than ever before.

In this part of your journal, you will look back and honestly reflect on your relationship experience. They say hindsight is 20/20. Knowing what you know now, use the next few pages to objectively look back at your relationship and choose what you want to take with you and what you want to leave behind!

RED FLAGS

Use this page to list (or draw) all the red flags you missed or ignored during your relationship.

WHAT I'LL MISS ABOUT THE RELATIONSHIP...

What I won't miss about the relationship...

"No relationship is ever a waste of your time. If it didn't bring you what you want, it taught you what you don't want."
—Unknown

My unmet needs/desires in the relationship:

ALL THE PLACES I SHRUNK DOWN...

We shrink ourselves down when we refrain from: standing up for ourselves, asking for what we need, or setting a necessary boundary.

All the times I gripped to the relationship...

Gripping looks like controlling, manipulating, or forcing an outcome due to fear of losing something.

If I were honest with myself from the start, here's what would be different:

WHAT CAN I TAKE RESPONSIBILITY FOR?

I AM PROUD OF MYSELF FOR...

WHAT I'M NOT SO PROUD OF, BUT I'M GLAD I'M SEEING NOW...

My positive contributions to the relationship:

WHAT I'M TAKING WITH ME…	WHAT I'M LEAVING BEHIND…

PART THREE:
REPAIR YOUR RELATIONSHIP WITH YOURSELF

"Owning our story and loving ourselves through that process is the bravest thing that we will ever do."
– *Brené Brown*

What if I were to tell you that you've already met the person you're going to spend the rest of your life with? It's true...that person is you! We often lose ourselves inside of relationships, whether we bend over backwards to accommodate the other person or we shut down and close our hearts to protect ourselves.

It's time to give yourself some LOVE, the kind of love you truly deserve. Once you start treating yourself with the exquisite care you'd give a work of art or a really expensive car, other people in your life will start treating you that way, too. Welcome back to you!

I FORGIVE MYSELF FOR...

WHAT DOES MY INNER CHILD NEED?

INNER CHILD DRAWING

Your inner child wants to play on this page! Take a crayon or colorful marker in your non-dominant hand, and allow your inner child to take over.

DRAW (OR LIST) YOUR SUPPORT SYSTEM

The people around you matter! Surround yourself with loving, understanding, and supportive humans only. No exceptions!

All the ways I'm awesome...

What makes you awesome? DM me on Instagram and let me know. Seriously... I want to celebrate with you.
@breakupbreakthrough

THESE ARE THINGS THAT BRING ME PLEASURE...

I AM MOST CONFIDENT WHEN...

What boundaries can I set to protect my heart and help me heal?

Boundaries are limits you set on your energy, time, and personal space that teach people how to treat you.

What I do for self-care:

What I'll do to take care of myself this week…

My idea of the perfect date...

> Guess what? You don't have to wait for someone else to take you on a hot date... put on your favorite outfit and take yourself out!

MY MANTRAS!

Use this space to write positive affirmations for yourself.

I am…

I deserve…

I can be…

I am worthy of…

Here's some space to create your own…

PART FOUR:
LETTING GO OF WHAT YOU NO LONGER NEED

"Letting go is teaching me that I'm not losing-- but receiving. I'm gaining knowledge, resilience, and room in my heart for something greater."

– Alex Elle

Part of living a powerful life is letting go of what no longer serves you. We human beings like to hold on to a lot: relationships, identities, possessions, ideas. In fact, we don't just hold on, we grip! And that gripping can be incredibly draining.

If you want something to change, it will take a commitment to letting go-- letting go of the things that are keeping you from evolving into the best version of yourself. While it can feel scary or uncomfortable to let go, liberation awaits on the other side. In this part of your journal, you're going to let go of some stuff, and you'll probably feel much lighter (and freer) when you do!

ALL THE PLANS & DREAMS THAT WON'T HAPPEN...

HERE'S WHAT I NEED TO LET GO OF...

THIS IS WHAT'S KEEPING ME FROM LETTING GO...

WHEN I LET GO OF THESE THINGS, IT WILL MAKE SPACE FOR…

RELEASING THESE THINGS WILL FEEL...

If nothing was holding me back, I would...

THIS IS WHAT I NEED TO CREATE CLOSURE FOR MYSELF...

I Forgive My Ex For...

Forgiveness is a gift you give, not to your ex, but to yourself. To forgive is to set yourself free.

A GOODBYE LETTER TO MY EX

Letting Go Ritual

A letting go ritual is a powerful way to close out your relationship. Some people like to take a piece of rope and physically "cut the cord". Other rituals may include burning the goodbye letter, tearing it up, locking it away, sharing it with a friend, making a video diary, etc. This ritual is yours. You get to create it however you want.

This is my letting go ritual...

PART FIVE:
MOVING FORWARD

"You have brains in your head. You have feet in your shoes. You can steer yourself any direction you choose. You're on your own. And you know what you know. And you are the one who'll decide where to go…"

— *Dr. Seuss*

You're over the hump! The hardest part is behind you. While you may still feel grief around your breakup, you're now starting to create space in your life. Every time we let go of something, we have a space where that thing once lived-- either energetically or physically.

In this part of your journal, you get to create your life exactly how you want it-- you get to fill up those spaces with projects, relationships, and experiences that will nourish you.

This is the fun part, so let's dive in!

These are my desires for today...

THESE ARE MY BIG DESIRES FOR THE FUTURE...

HERE'S WHAT I WANT TO CREATE FOR MY FUTURE...

HERE'S WHAT I WANT TO BRING INTO MY LIFE…

I WANT TO POUR MY ENERGY INTO...

If I wasn't afraid, I would...

THESE ARE MY NON-NEGOTIABLES FOR FUTURE RELATIONSHIPS...

How I want to feel in my next relationship...

> "Knowing how you actually want to feel is the most potent form of clarity that you can have."
> —Danielle LaPorte

A LETTER TO MY FUTURE PARTNER:

LOVING REMINDERS TO MYSELF...

WHAT'S NEXT?

Congratulations on starting your breakup breakthrough journey with this journal. There's so much community, love, support, and gifts waiting for you at

www.breakupbreakthrough.com/journal

I'll see you there!

About the Author

Paige is a breakup coach and the founder of Breakup Breakthrough.

After experiencing a particularly devastating breakup that left her feeling like she had failed at yet another relationship, Paige knew something needed to change. So she set out on a journey to fall in love with *herself*, and that's exactly what she did.

She spent a year saying *yes* to her desires, shattering unhealthy patterns, and recreating her life on *her* terms. Now, she's on a mission to help people look at their breakups, not as failures, but as opportunities for growth. She is committed to helping people turn heartbreaking experiences into breakthroughs, so they can feel confident and empowered to create the future of their dreams.

Learn more at www.breakupbreakthrough.com

Follow Paige on Instagram @breakupbreakthrough

CPSIA information can be obtained
at www.ICGtesting.com
Printed in the USA
LVHW080954061220
673148LV00046B/935